WORLDWIDE ADVENTURE

Robert Abel

Valentine Publishing House
Denver, Colorado

All Rights Reserved
Copyright © 2010 by Robert Abel
No part of this book may be reproduced or transmitted in any form or by any
means, electronic or mechanical, including photocopying or recording, without
written permission from the publisher, except in the case of brief quotations
embodied in religious articles and reviews. For permission, please contact:

Valentine Publishing House LLC
P.O. Box 27422
Denver, Colorado 80227

The Scripture quotations contained herein are from the New Revised Standard
Version Bible: Catholic Edition copyright © 1993 and 1989 by the Division of
Christian Education of the National Council of the Churches of Christ in the
U.S.A. Used by permission. All rights reserved.

Cover Graphics—Desert Isle Design LLC

Publisher's Cataloging-in-Publication Data

Abel, Robert.
    Worldwide Adventure / Robert Abel

        p. : ill. ; cm.

    ISBN–10: 0-9796331-6-8
    ISBN–13: 978-0-9796331-6-4
    Includes bibliographical references.

1. Catholic Church. 2. Church renewal—Religious aspects—Christianity.
3. Evangelization—Religious aspects—Christianity. I. Title.

BX1746 .A24 2010
282

Printed in the United States of America.

*"To the one who conquers
I will give a place with me on my throne,
just as I myself conquered and sat
down with my Father on his throne.
Let anyone who has an ear listen to what
the Spirit is saying to the churches."*

Revelation 3:21–22

CHAPTER ONE

The adventure began one day in church, I was sitting in the back row thinking there had to be more to the Christian walk than what I was experiencing. Saint Paul, one of the greatest missionaries of all time, lived an exciting adventure with the Lord. In the book of Acts, Paul and Barnabas moved with such a mighty outpouring of God's Spirit that the townspeople wanted to offer sacrifices to them.

After speaking boldly about the Lord and working a vast number of signs and wonders in Iconium, Paul and Barnabas traveled to Lystra. When they entered the city, *there was a man sitting who could not use his feet and had never walked, for he had been crippled from birth. He listened to Paul as he was speaking. And Paul, looking at him intently and seeing that he had faith to be healed, said in a loud voice, "Stand upright on your feet." And the man sprang up and began to walk.*

When the crowds saw what Paul had done, they shouted in the Lycaonian language, "The gods have come down to us in human form!" Barnabas they called Zeus, and Paul they called Hermes, because he was the chief speaker. The priest of Zeus, whose temple was just outside the city, brought oxen and garlands to the gates; he and the crowds wanted to offer sacrifice.[1]

When the apostles Barnabas and Paul heard of it, they tore their clothes and rushed out into the crowd, shouting, "Friends, why are you doing this? We are mortals just like you, and we bring you good news, that you should turn from these worthless things to the living God, who made the heaven and the earth and the sea and all that is in them. Even with these words, they scarcely restrained the crowds from offering sacrifice to them.[2]

On anther occasion, Paul and Barnabas stirred up such a commotion that the Jews from Antioch and Iconium tried to kill them. In Acts 14:19–20, *they stoned Paul and dragged him out of the city, supposing that he was dead. But when the disciples surrounded him, he got up and went into the city. The next day he went on with Barnabas to Derbe.* Town after town, Paul and Barnabas were unstoppable. They lived an exciting adventure with the Lord—moving with God's power while accomplishing God's will in some of the most challenging and difficult ministry assignments imaginable.

As I continued meditating on the life of the apostles, I felt trapped in a state of churchgoing complacency. I had a desire to move with God's power just like Paul and Barnabas, but I felt hindered as if my true potential was slowly wasting away, being consumed by the worries and cares of everyday life.

That's when I began to pray, "God, get me out of here!"

I had enough airline miles to book a flight to Africa and even had clergy contacts in both Lagos, Nigeria, and Kissi, Kenya. The pastor from Nigeria seemed more receptive to a visit and was extremely helpful when it came time to set up a schedule of ministry assignments. Even though I had a desire to set out on the adventure of a lifetime, my fleshly desires were constantly interfering. The first objection was the interruption of my daily routine. Did I really want to spend 20 hours in and out of airports? I had to fly from Denver to Chicago, from Chicago to Frankfurt, and from Frankfurt to Lagos. Another objective was spending my airline miles on a mission trip, when I could be spending them on at least two vacations to a tropical island.

I asked a few friends to join me, but everybody made the same excuse about their finances—not being able to afford the airfare, and not being able to take time off work.

Another issue was related to my personal safety. According to the U.S. government *Travel Warning*, Nigeria was extremely dangerous: *Visitors to Nigeria, including American citizens, have been victims of armed robbery on the airport roads from Lagos and Abuja during both daylight and nighttime hours. Some visitors and resident Americans have experienced armed muggings, assaults, burglary, kidnappings, and extortion, often involving violence, as well as carjackings, roadblock robberies, and armed break-ins.[3]*

Violent crime committed by individuals and gangs, as well as by some persons wearing police and military uniforms, is an ongoing problem, especially at night. Crime is particularly acute in Lagos. Traveling outside of major cities during hours of darkness is not recommended due to both crime and road safety concerns.[4]

After conducting more research into the potential threats, I found out that criminals would congregate outside the airport to watch for kidnap victims. Traveling at night was dangerous because gang members with machine guns would lay barricades across the road to stop cars. Once the victim's car came to a complete stop, the robbers would place another obstruction behind the vehicle to prevent the victim from backing up. Even the flight crews were at risk. In the event that a flight crew needed to spend the night in Lagos, they were not allowed to leave the airport without an armed security guard.

Another concern was the health risk. Malaria is caused by a parasite that lays eggs in a person's liver. Once the eggs hatch and the parasites start bursting red blood cells, the infected person will get very sick. Mosquitoes can also carry a parasitic worm, that when transmitted to humans, can cause severe swelling known as elephantiasis. If this condition is left untreated, the infected person's body parts can swell up to two or three times their normal size.

While conducting more research into the health risks, I also found out that African sleeping sickness is caused by a bite from an infected tsetse fly. Once the parasite from the fly enters a person's body, it can cause fever, swelling of the face and hands, headaches, fatigue, aching muscles, and swollen lymph nodes. When the parasites multiply and start attacking the person's central nervous system, that person will experience progressive confusion, personality changes, daytime sleepiness, and other neurological problems.

Over the next several months I continued praying about my personal safety and health risks. There were more than enough fleshly, fear-driven concerns to discourage my plans. But then again, another part of me wanted to live an exciting adventure with the Lord. I wanted a move with God's power while fulfilling the Great Commission. In Matthew 28:18–20, Jesus said, *"All authority in heaven and on earth has been given to me. Go therefore and make disciples of all nations, baptizing them in the name of the Father and of the Son and of the Holy Spirit, and teaching them to obey everything that I have commanded you. And remember, I am with you always, to the end of the age."*

If Jesus wanted me to embark on the adventure of a lifetime, I didn't have anything to fear. If Jesus was calling me, he would also accompany me. The question was, did the Lord want me to go on a mission trip in the first place? If so, should I go to Kenya or Nigeria? The people in both countries speak English, and there's extreme poverty in both places. According to U.S. government statistics, the average citizen in Nigeria earns $6.03 per day, and in Kenya, the average citizen earns $4.93 per day.

As I continued to pray about the mission trip, I could hear the Lord say, "Yes" when I asked his permission to visit Nigeria.

CHAPTER TWO

Before I set out for the adventure of a lifetime, I sent the pastor from Nigeria enough money to buy 1,200 pounds of rice and seeds for the villagers to grow crops. I also loaded several bags with candy for the kids, vitamins, and medical supplies to take with me on the plane. It was my intention to rent a van, and after loading it with supplies, I wanted to visit as many villages as possible before returning to Ajido to conduct an AIDS awareness seminar and healing service.

Upon my arrival, I was able to put together a small ministry team that consisted of our van driver, an associate pastor named John, a lay evangelist named Bunmi, and several others. After meeting at my hotel around 9:00 a.m., we set out for the first village in two vehicles. The road leading to the village was rough and dusty. As we approached the location, I could see a bamboo shade canopy in the distance with several rows of plastic chairs. It looked like the villagers had been using the structure for a church.

When we came to a stop, a young man came running up to the vehicle to greet us. Our van driver called him the "man-on-ground," because he was the missionary in charge of the area. It was his responsibility to gather the people for our arrival. According to the man-on-ground, the village had already been notified the day before, and they were expecting us at 11:00 a.m.

Because we were an hour early, Bunmi told me to have a seat. She wanted to wait an hour for the people to arrive. Almost immediately, I could feel anger rising up inside of me. I looked at the other pastors and said, "I thought we weren't going to do any staged events."

"What do you mean?" one pastor asked.

"I didn't spend 20 hours coming here to conduct a staged event," I said, pointing at the bamboo structure. "You call this ministry—gathering Christians from the village so that we can talk about the Lord?"

"What's wrong with that?" Bunmi asked.

"It cost a lot of money to come here," I said. "I didn't come all this way to talk with a handful of Christians about Christ. Where are the Muslims or the idol worshipers?"

"Muslims live in the village across the highway," the man-on-ground said.

After saying a prayer, we divided into three groups. Two teams would walk around the Christian village and invite people to the staged event. Associate

Pastor John, the man-on-ground, and I would cross the highway and speak with the Muslims. On our way to the Muslim camp, we passed several bamboo shacks. There were many chickens running around, along with several people peering out at us from their doorways. As we passed by, we invited them to the staged event by saying, "Please come, we want to give you presents."

After crossing the two-lane road separated by a deep median, we entered the Muslim camp and came upon a group of 30 men playing cards. It looked like they were gambling. Several of them were playing musical instruments, and others were talking and laughing. After interrupting them to get their attention, I invited them to the staged event by saying, "Hi, we're Christians, we love Muslims, and we would like to invite you to our church service."

As soon as I said the word *Christian* one man became very aggressive. He started shouting at the others in a language that I couldn't understand. It looked like he was trying to incite the others to violence. When I tried to communicate with him, he wouldn't look me in the eyes. He just kept shouting at his friends. The man-on-ground started backing away, but Pastor John stood next to me like a rock. He kept trying to talk with them.

Right before the mission trip, I spent a lot of time studying Islam. The northern part of Nigeria is predominately Muslim, and the southern part is mostly Christian. There is a state in the middle of the country called Jos, where extreme violence had been occurring. Several weeks before my arrival, Muslims were in the process of building a mosque, when Christian schoolchildren started a protest.

After a full-scale riot broke out, the Muslims and Christians started fighting each other with machetes. Hundreds of people were admitted to the hospital, and many others died. Because these types of conflicts were common in Nigeria, tensions between Christians and Muslims were already running high. It was apparent that we were interrupting their card game and starting to make them mad. I could feel the hostile attitude rising, until finally one man said, "I would like to hear what you have to say."

"Very good," I said. "Everyone who wants to hear what we have to say, please come over here." About 20 men stood up and followed us to a location about 50 feet away from the card game.

I began by taking a copy of the Koran from my backpack. This was the first time I had the opportunity to deliver a message to a Muslim audience, and I didn't know what to expect. I was caught up in the excitement of the moment. I could sense a lot of hostility, so I began by saying, "The Koran says 11 times that Jesus is the Messiah."

One man from the Muslim camp started translating on my behalf into the villagers' native language. He would repeat the words I was saying, but then he would add his own commentary by saying things like, "We don't believe that Jesus is the Son of God."

The hostile attitude continued to grow, until I said, "We're not here to convert anyone to Christianity. All we want to do is share about the Messiah, because the penalty for sin is death."

As soon as I told them we were not there to convert anyone, the tensions settled down. I was able to share with them from the Koran how God removed all sinful men from the face of the earth during the great flood, and that only one righteous man named Noah along with his family survived. After establishing that the penalty for sin is death, I gave everyone a choice—they could pay the death penalty themselves or allow the Messiah to pay the death penalty on their behalf.

During the 30-minute conversation, a few men wandered away, but at the end, we were able to pray with at least 12 men who accepted the Messiah's sacrifice on the cross for the forgiveness of their sins. After promising to bring back sacks of rice, the man-on-ground received a call on his cell phone. The other pastors were looking for us. The bamboo shade pavilion had filled with people, and they wanted us to come back and deliver an encouraging message.

Because most of the people gathered around the stage were Christians, I encouraged them to go deeper with the Lord. I challenged them to spend time every day practicing contemplative prayer, so they could ask God questions about their lives and listen for his answers. Once they received an answer to one of their questions, they would need to proceed forth in obedience. Step-by-step, this three-part process would transform their lives.

CHAPTER THREE

After delivering an encouraging message to the Christians, we gave away two hundred pounds of rice along with instructions about the use of vitamins. We also gave the villagers seeds so they could grow crops and gave candy to the children.

One woman from a nearby village had a sick child. She said her baby seemed lifeless compared to other children, and he didn't have a desire to move around. She wanted us to pray for healing, so I asked her, "Has your baby been baptized?"

"We don't do that here," one of the pastors said.

"I know you don't, but if I show you in the Bible, will you stand in agreement with me?" I asked.

"Yes," the pastor said.

"The problem is that the baby is too small to accept Jesus as his savior. Why wait until the child reaches the age of reason to invite the Holy Spirit, when we can do it right now?" I said.

Because the mother didn't speak English, the pastors had to translate for me. Pointing to the woman, I said, "Please ask her if she has been baptized." The answer that came back was "No, she has not been baptized." She came from a pagan background, had never denounced her occult-like practices, and had never accepted Jesus as her savior.

"We can pray all we want," I said, "but unless we deal with the underlying issues, our prayers for healing may not produce favorable results. The first step is to get the woman to denounce the devil and all forms of occult-like practices. Next, she needs to choose Jesus as her savior and be filled with the Holy Spirit. After the woman enters into an authentic relationship with Christ, she can then dedicate her child to God. After we invite the Holy Spirit to dwell inside the little boy's body through baptism, we can lay hands on him and command the demonic illness to never again return.

"Do you agree with this?" I asked.

"Yes," the pastors said.

I spent the next 20 minutes teaching the pastors about infant baptism. I began by showing them how the prophet Samuel was filled with the Holy Spirit at a very early age. In Luke 1:15, John the Baptist was filled with the Holy Spirit inside his mother's womb. We also studied Acts 2:37 when Peter preached a sermon to 3,000 families. During his discourse Peter said, *"Repent, and be baptized every one of you in the name of Jesus Christ so that your sins may be forgiven; and you will receive the gift of the Holy Spirit. For the promise is for you, for your children, and for all who are far away, everyone whom the Lord our God calls to him."*[5]

"Why would you want your children to go unprotected?" I asked. "Most Christians wait until their children are in grade school before they accept Jesus, then afterward, they want to be filled with the Holy Spirit. Why wait, when God has provided a way for children to receive the Holy Spirit through baptism?"

Because there were no more objections, we asked the mother to denounce Satan along with all his evil works and to choose Jesus as her savior. After baptizing the mother, we joined in agreement with her, as she consecrated her baby to God. After baptizing the little boy with a bottle of water, we asked for the impartation of the Holy Spirit and commanded all forms of demonic illness to get out of the little boy's body.

I didn't bring a copy of the Catechism with me, and even if I did, the Protestant pastors wouldn't have paid too much attention to what it said, but according to section 1265, *Baptism not only purifies from all sins, but also makes the neophyte a new creature, an adopted son of God, who has become a partaker of the divine nature, member of Christ and co-heir with him, and a temple of the Holy Spirit.*[6]

The Catechism also says in section 1256, *In case of necessity, anyone, even a non-baptized person, with the required intention, can baptize, by using the Trinitarian baptismal formula.*[7] It also says that *the parents would deny a child the priceless grace of becoming a child of God were they not to confer Baptism shortly after birth.*[8]

Because of the high infant-mortality rate in Africa, combined with the lack of solid biblical teaching, the need to baptize small children has become more than a necessity, it is a requirement. According to John 3:5, *No one can enter the kingdom of God without being born of water and Spirit.* Baptism is also a required part of the Great Commission when Jesus said, *"All authority in heaven and on earth has been given to me. Go therefore and make disciples of all nations, baptizing them in the name of the Father and of the Son and of the Holy Spirit, and teaching them to obey everything that I have commanded you."[9]*

After baptizing the woman and her baby, we rushed off to the next village. It took us over an hour to get there, because of the rough and dusty roads. The houses in this farming village were made mostly of a red-colored clay, other structures were built from cinder blocks. The majority of the homes had gravestones next to them, as if the residents wanted to be close to their deceased loved ones.

Our first stop was to see the village chief. We wanted to share with him our intentions and receive his blessing. After receiving the chief's approval, we teamed up with one of Bunmi's missionary friends, who had spent a lot of time working in the area. After we prayed and divided into teams, I spent most of my time talking with a Muslim scholar. He used to be very radical when he was younger, but some type of paralysis had settled into his body, making it hard for him to move around.

He listened very intently to the message about the Messiah and about our need to accept his sacrifice on the cross for the forgiveness of our sins. Right before we prayed together, I asked him to picture a jail cell. "Because we have all sinned and fallen short, I want you to close your eyes and picture what your own execution would look like. Can you do that?" I asked.

"Yes," he said.

"Now picture the Messiah unlocking the jail cell door. Picture him sitting down next to you and saying, 'I will pay the death penalty on your behalf. All you have to do is walk through the door and go free.'"

"Will you do that?" I asked.

"Yes," the man said.

"Very good," I said. "Before you walk through the jail cell door to go free, I want you to thank the Messiah in your own words."

During my prayer time with the scholar, I was careful not to pray for things on his behalf. God wanted this man to ask for his own healing, not for him to sit there and watch me do it for him. The scholar needed to use his own free will to accept the Messiah's sacrifice on the cross for the forgiveness of his sins. Once he entered into an authentic relationship with God, we then had the power to command all forms of demonic illness to leave his body.

After praying with the Muslim scholar and his family, I gave them several packages of seeds so they could grow crops, before meeting up with the other pastors who had gathered in the village square. Apparently, there had been many sudden deaths in the village with an above-average infant-mortality rate, so one of the pastors felt the need to pray against the spirit of death. Several Muslim men had gathered to watch us pray, but they didn't say anything, nor did they seem interested in joining with us in prayer. I heard later that the Muslims in this village didn't allow any type of public Christian prayer, but this day, they seemed to have made an exception.

The needs were so great that we could have spent several days in the area, but after dropping off two bags of rice for Bunmi's friend to distribute, we rushed off to our next appointment. My only regret was not being able to spend more time with the people. I would have liked several follow-up appointments with the Muslim scholar, but I felt better after hearing a report several weeks later that his health and mobility had been steadily improving.

CHAPTER FOUR

The next day, after ministering to several hundred people who had gathered in a church, we boarded two boats in the afternoon and set out across the water. Because it was late in the day, we needed to spend the night in one of the villages. There were four villages altogether, one was Christian, two were Muslim, and the other village was mixed.

Before arriving at the Muslim village, I heard one of the evangelists say that he tried to show the *Jesus* film there a year ago, but the villagers grew violent and kicked him and his companions out. When I heard this, I asked our boat driver to stop the engine so that we could pray. Slowly, we drifted across the deep-blue, calm water. Because we were close to shore, I didn't want the sound of our voices to carry across the water, so we all prayed quietly for the salvation of souls.

As we approached the boat dock, I saw several men sitting underneath a covered pavilion. After greeting them, I asked to speak to the village chief.

They took me to a tall, thin man who agreed to gather his community together to hear the message. As the villagers were gathering underneath the shade of a tall tree, I felt the need to go back to the boat dock to invite anybody else who might want to join us.

When I started walking away, two pastors ran after me calling out, "Where are you going?" They followed me down the path, and one pastor begin translating my words to those who had been left behind. The other pastor kept projecting fear on me. He kept saying things like, "Be very careful—they kicked us out of here last year." I was feeling enough anxiety without him making it worse, so I looked him in the eyes and said, "I denounce all fear in the name of Jesus."

After rounding up the last of the villagers, there were about 80 people gathered underneath a large tree. I gave them the same message as before. After establishing that the penalty for sin is death, I gave everyone the opportunity to pay the death penalty themselves or allow the Messiah to pay it on their behalf. One by one, I pointed to everyone in the crowd, and they all wanted to accept the Messiah's sacrifice on the cross for the forgiveness of their sins.

At one point in our prayer time, a young man who appeared to be the imam, or spiritual leader for the community, said a prayer that everybody else repeated. Because the Koran in sura 58:22 talks about a need to be strengthened with God's Spirit, we also prayed for the infilling of the Holy Spirit. When it came time for the pastors to distribute the rice, I handed a bottle of vitamins to the village chief. He seemed very interested in them, so I said, "These will be good for sick people."

"Can you take them if you're not sick?" he asked.

"Yes," I said. "The tablets contain all the necessary vitamins and minerals that your body needs. They will help you stay healthy."

After distributing our gifts, everybody in the village followed us to the boat dock and waved good-bye as we set out across the water to our next location. By now, the end of the day was quickly approaching, and I was feeling emotionally and spiritually drained. We had one more stop to make, and I didn't want to do any more ministry.

As we approached the shore, I noticed all the villagers had gathered on the waterfront with musical instruments. They were singing songs of praise and followed us into their church. Even though I didn't have any strength left, as soon as I started addressing the villagers, the Holy Spirit took over, and once again, I felt empowered.

After completing all of our ministry assignments, I had a free day to rest and recover. I had the opportunity to either spend a day at the beach or go for another day of ministry work. After thinking about my options, I called Bunmi and asked her to borrow a car so we could visit several more villages. It was nonstop action and excitement as thousands of people's lives were transformed.

CHAPTER FIVE

The apostles also shared this same kind of excitement when they embarked on a mission trip. In Luke 9:1–2, *Jesus called the twelve together and gave them power and authority over all demons and to cure diseases, and he sent them out to proclaim the kingdom of God and to heal.* In Luke 10:1, Jesus sent out 70 others with the same instructions. They were to heal the sick, proclaim the good news, and cast out demons.

The seventy returned with joy, saying, "Lord, in your name even the demons submit to us!" He said to them, "I watched Satan fall from heaven like a flash of lightning. See, I have given you authority to tread on snakes and scorpions, and over all the power of the enemy; and nothing will hurt you." [10]

If the 12 apostles in Luke 9 represent the priesthood, then the 70 disciples in Luke 10 would represent the laity. According to the Catechism, *Those who accepted Jesus' message to follow him are called his disciples.* [11] To better understand the laity's role in becoming the Lord's disciples, it will be helpful to define the following terms—*Believer, Disciple, Apostle,* and *Apostolate.*

Believer

A believer is someone who believes in God. Somewhere in every believer's past that person has had an encounter with God, and from that point forward, they are able to believe in God's existence. Other forms of believers include those who raise their hands during an altar call in an attempt to believe that Jesus will save them.

Disciple

A disciple is one who applies the Lord's teachings to his life. The process of becoming a disciple usually requires many years of sanctification and cooperation with the Holy Spirit in a way that transforms men into new creatures in Christ. The process of becoming a disciple involves dying to self, leaving behind worldly ways, and obedience to the Lord's will.

Apostle

The word *apostle* comes from the Greek, meaning one who is sent. The Catechism defines apostle as *one who is sent as Jesus was sent by the Father.*[12] After a man has applied the teachings of Christ to his life by becoming a disciple, he is then required to share the same teachings with others. As the Father sent Jesus into the world to teach us how to live, so too does Jesus send forth his followers to make disciples of all nations. Anyone who is sent by Jesus to carry on the missionary activity of the Church is considered to be an apostle.

Apostolate

According to the Catechism, an apostolate is *the activity of the Christian which fulfills the apostolic nature of the whole Church by working to extend the reign of Christ to the entire world.*[13] An apostolate is just another name for a lay person's missionary activities. If after applying the Lord's teaching to your life, Jesus calls you into ministry, then the work you do for the Lord is your apostolate.

Even though the Bible and Catechism call the Christian faithful into the Lord's service, there seems to be a large majority of Catholics who fail to use their spiritual gifts. Many parishioners may not even feel like they have any spiritual gifts, and others may have tried serving the Lord in the past, but after experiencing some form of hardship, they have given up.

There also seems to be a stifling form of complacency in some churches, where the laity are not allowed to do anything except serve as a ushers or Eucharistic ministers or sing in the choir.

In an attempt to address these problems and empower the laity, a council of over 2,500 bishops gathered together in Rome to draft a document entitled *Apostolicam Actuositatem—Decree on the Apostolate of Lay People.* In this document, a Sacred Assembly of Bishops under the direction of Pope Paul VI, start out by saying, *In its desire to intensify the apostolic activity of the People of God the Council now earnestly turns its thoughts to the Christian laity. Mention has already been made in other documents of the laity's special and indispensable role in the mission of the Church. Indeed, the Church can never be without the lay apostolate; it is something that derives from the layman's very vocation as a Christian.[14]*

From the fact of their union with Christ the head flows the laymen's right and duty to be apostles. Inserted as they are in the Mystical Body of Christ by baptism and strengthened by the power of the Holy Spirit in confirmation, it is by the Lord himself that they are assigned to the apostolate.[15]

The need for this urgent and many-sided apostolate is shown by the manifest action of the Holy Spirit moving laymen today to a deeper and deeper awareness of their responsibility and urging them on everywhere to the service of Christ and the Church.[16]

In an attempt to help the laity gain a better understanding of their responsibilities in serving Christ and the Church, the bishops have provided clarification for the lay apostolate using the following categories—Evangelization and Sanctification, Renewal of the Temporal Order, and Charitable Works and Social Aid.

Evangelization and Sanctification

Evangelization and sanctification have been linked together because both are required elements for making disciples of all nations. For many Catholics, the word *evangelization* may seem like Protestant terminology. During my work with the homeless, I have met many well-intentioned Christians who consider themselves evangelists. Many of them go around trying to save other people. They think that by getting others to believe that Jesus will save them, that somehow they will be granted access to heaven one day.

For many Protestant evangelicals, the process works similar to cognitive therapy. If the evangelist can get a man to think or believe that he will be saved, then somehow Jesus will look into that man's thoughts at the end of his life, and after identifying his mental beliefs, his sins will be forgiven and he will be saved.

From the Catholic perspective, evangelization is entirely different because it requires sanctification as well as the need to teach everything that Jesus taught. At the center of Catholic evangelization resides the Gospel message, but there is more to salvation than just raising your hand during an altar call. True conversion requires a person to be baptized, to be filled with the Holy Spirit, and to embrace the process of sanctification. Because an authentic Christian walk will require a turning away from sins, surrendering of self-willed ways, and obedience to the Lord, a Catholic lay evangelist will need to be able to live, teach, and impart all these qualities to others.

The work of a Catholic lay evangelist not only applies to those outside the Church, but it also applies to those inside the Church. According to the bishops' decree, *Laymen have countless opportunities for exercising the apostolate of evangelization and sanctification. The very witness of a Christian life, and good works done in a supernatural spirit, are effective in drawing men to the faith and to God; and that is what the Lord has said: "Your light must shine so brightly before men that they can see your good works and glorify your Father who is in heaven."*[17]

This witness of life, however, is not the sole element

in the apostolate; the true apostle is on the lookout for occasions of announcing Christ by word, either to unbelievers to draw them towards the faith, or to the faithful to instruct them, strengthen them, incite them to a more fervent life.[18]

Renewal of the Temporal Order

According to the bishops' decree, the temporal order consists of everything that makes up our world: *Personal and family values, culture, economic interests, the trades and professions, institutions of the political community, international relations, and so on, as well as their gradual development.*[19] In other words, the laity have been given the responsibility to renew every aspect of our society, government, and world. The clergy are responsible for everything that takes place within the Church, and the laity have been given the responsibility for the renewal of the entire temporal order.

A good example of the laity's need to renew the temporal order comes from a time when I signed a contract to purchase a small parcel of land. My intention was to buy the property and build a subdivision of townhouse units. The property was located in a well-established, middle-class neighborhood. Many of the ranch-style homes to the east of the property were situated on oversized lots and surrounded by mature trees. To the south of the property, a smaller two-story building was being used as a school for special needs children. The same company that operated the school also owned a white commercial building directly to the north that they were using for their administrative staff.

After conducting some preliminary research, I felt inspired to submit a full-price offer. The contract contained a clause giving me 12 months to obtain the necessary zoning approval and also required a $5,000 earnest deposit. Several days after submitting the contract, I received a phone call from my real estate agent who said, "Congratulations, the sellers have accepted your offer."

"That's great news," I said. "I may have also found an investor for the project."

"Very good," Mike said. "You have 12 months to work out the details."

CHAPTER SIX

Because I wanted to rezone the property from commercial to residential, the county would require me to notify all the homeowner associations within a five-mile radius of the property. Before I sent the letters out, I wanted to meet my neighbors personally to introduce myself and explain the project. I began one day knocking on doors of the homes behind the vacant lot. When an older gentleman answered the first door, he said, "You're not part of that Shiloh Group, are you?"

"I think they own the school and office building on either side of the vacant lot," I said, "but I've never met them. Why? What's wrong with the Shiloh Group?"

"I personally don't have anything against them, but there are a lot of folks around here that do."

"They seem very quiet," I said. "There's only a few cars in the parking lot during the day. Little kids making noise at the school next door shouldn't be a problem, besides I'm planning to build a fence around the property, so that it will be a self-enclosed community."

After speaking with my neighbor for about an hour, it felt like we were starting to develop a friendship. He didn't have a problem with me building residential homes on the property, in fact, he liked the idea better than a commercial building with exterior lights that might shine through his windows at night.

After knocking on a few more doors, I found most of the people very receptive to having a housing project built on the other side of the fence. One man wanted me to plant large pine trees behind his house, but other than that, everybody seemed to like the idea.

The next day, I decided to stop by the Shiloh Group to share my plans about the housing project. When I entered the white, one-story stucco building, I was greeted by a friendly receptionist who asked me to have a seat in the waiting area. Within a few minutes, I was greeted by a middle-aged man who said, "Hi, my name is Mr. George. How can I assist you?"

"I have a contract to purchase the lot next door, and I wanted to introduce myself and share my plans with you."

When Mr. George looked at the site plan, he appeared a little concerned. When I asked him about his objections, he said, "I have experienced a lot of problems from the homeowners in this area. The thought of another homeowner's association between my school and office building doesn't sound very appealing."

"Why? What happened between you and the homeowners?" I asked.

"We have been in business for over 25 years, providing housing and treatment for juvenile sex offenders. We used to have a great relationship with the homeowner's association and many other residents in this area. Then one day, they accused me of lying and taking advantage of the kids."

"What happened?" I asked.

"Many of the residents used to reach out and befriend our kids. The homeowner's association used to host Christmas and Halloween parties. Then one day they accused me of using the kids to get rich. Others started spreading lies. After we had an incident where one of the teenage boys was caught sneaking out the window at night, an angry mob formed. They egged cars in my parking lot and even sent death threats."

"Are your kids living in this neighborhood now?" I asked.

"We are currently renting a duplex and have four other single-family residences. According to zoning, we are allowed to have six children in one home, and they are supervised 24 hours a day by my staff."

As we continued talking about the daily operations of his ministry, Mr. George's eyes welled up with tears when he described the hardship that some of his kids had been through. One boy was only seven years old when Social Services removed him from his home. Mr. George said that the little guy used to cry himself to sleep for months, because he missed his parents.

Apparently, he had been caught molesting one of his neighborhood friends. When the other boy's parents found out, they pressed charges and were able to pressure the court to have him removed from his house.

As Mr. George described the situation, it sounded like the seven-year-old boy had been molested himself, and that he was only reacting out of the hurt that he had learned from others. Because everybody is created in the image and likeness of God, it's very doubtful that God would create a little boy to be a child molester.

In another situation, a 17-year-old boy was having sex with his girlfriend, but when the girl's parents found out, they accused the boy of rape and pressed charges against him. Not only was the young man instantly removed from his home by Social Services, but now he has to register as a sex offender for the rest of his life.

As Mr. George continued describing the hardships that his kids had been through, it was very evident that he loved them dearly and was doing his best to help them work through many difficult and challenging issues. After speaking with Mr. George for over an hour, I felt very comfortable with his ministry and didn't see a problem building residential housing next to his office and school.

CHAPTER SEVEN

When it came time to conduct my first public zoning meeting, about 15 people showed up. After I addressed my neighbors' concerns, everyone appeared to be very happy with the proposed residential development. Several of the homeowners behind the property wanted me to replace the fence, but other than that, there were no objections.

Over the next several months, the project continued moving forward, but for some reason, I had a growing feeling that it wouldn't be right to build residential housing in a commercial area. The more I prayed about the project, the more I felt the Lord wanted me to work with the Shiloh Group. If Mr. George moved his kids out of the residential neighborhood, it would make a lot of people very happy. Plus it would also save the Shiloh Group a lot of money. Instead of renting a duplex and four single-family homes to shelter six kids per house, the Shiloh Group could consolidate their operation into one centralized commercial facility.

There would also be the added benefit of reducing the number of staff required to supervise the kids. Instead of paying 12 staff members to monitor six different houses, Shiloh Group would save money monitoring the kids in one location. Building a commercial housing unit for Mr. George's kids seemed like the perfect use for the property. That way all his buildings would be next door to each other. Staff members could walk from the office building to the residential housing building to the school next door.

As I continued praying about the Lord's will for the property, I kept getting a sense that the property belonged to the Shiloh Group. After coming to this conclusion, I called my real estate agent and Mr. George to set up an appointment. Upon entering his office, we were greeted by Mr. George and his wife who invited us to sit down and discuss the proposal further. We spent several hours discussing all the options of a new commercial building. Mr. George wanted a big kitchen, a recreation room for his kids to play in, a conference room for his staff, and enough bedrooms for all his kids.

"It shouldn't be a problem," I said. "According to the existing site plan, we are allowed to build a 5,500 square-foot building next door."

"What about zoning?" Mr. George asked.

"The county has already approved the footprint for a commercial building. All we need to do is submit construction plans, and we can obtain a building permit within a few weeks. Because the property is not zoned for a sex-offender facility, we would need to get a variance from the county, which would require a public meeting," I said.

"That means it could start all over again," Mrs. George said, reaching out for her husband's hand.

"I don't think it will be a problem," I said. "The neighbors I spoke with were very nice."

"You haven't met the opposition group," Mr. George said.

"I think the majority of the neighborhood would like to see you move out of the single-family units and into a commercial property. If I went door to door, I'm sure I could find at least 100 supporters for the plan."

"Let's proceed with caution," Mr. George said, as we concluded our meeting.

I began by calling the county commissioner's office to set up several appointments. I wanted to hear the commissioner's thoughts before proceeding with a sex-offender facility. I had heard the county was already in the process of conducting public meetings for a government-run facility, so I met with two of the commissioners at separate times, and both seemed very positive about the Shiloh Group proposal.

The next day, I started calling members of the opposition group. I was able to set up an appointment with one lady named Jan. When I told her about Shiloh Group's plans, she became very agitated. I tried to get her to share her feelings, but all she kept saying was, "We'll have to see about that!"

The rest of the phone calls were not very productive. Several of the women started screaming profanities at me and saying things like, "Those little monsters are dangerous! We won't stop until the Shiloh Group is permanently removed from our neighborhood!" The conversations were so heated that I had to ask several of the women if they had been sexually abused in the past, and three of them acknowledged that they had been raped.

Over the next several weeks, the opposition group went into full force. They started calling property owners in the neighborhood in an attempt to spread distorted information about the kids in the program. I had a great relationship with the owners of a Christian school located up the street, but after members of the opposition group started threatening them, they wanted me to go back to the residential housing plan.

Apparently, the women were portraying the juvenile sex-offenders as stalkers who would sneak into the school during the day and rape young girls in the bathroom. They even threatened to contact the parents and conduct a public protest in front of the school.

The opposition group also called the county commissioner's office to make obscene remarks and complaints. It got so bad, that one of the commissioners called me in for a meeting. He told me about the public hearings that were taking place concerning the government-run facility and encouraged me to stop by the courthouse to see for myself. Apparently, there had been such a large turnout that the officials had to keep extending the hearing dates so that everybody would have a chance to testify.

Because the next hearing date was scheduled for Wednesday evening, I called my real estate agent and made plans to attend. Upon entering the hearing room, we noticed several public officials seated in front with their heads bowed toward the floor. Everybody who wanted to comment on the project was allowed three minutes. One-by-one, members from the audience were called to the podium.

One woman kept screaming hysterically that the sex offenders would molest her horse and other farm animals. Another man complained the government-run facility would diminish his property value. Another woman begged the officials not to let sex offenders in her neighborhood, because she had a five-year-old daughter at home. Others were concerned the sex offenders would attack the family dog and give it herpes.

Mike and I could only listen for about 20 minutes before leaving the room. Once we walked out the door, I cried out, "No way, I don't want to go through that!"

Over the next several weeks, Mike slowly lost interest in helping with the project. When it came time to conduct my first public meeting, he said, "I'm sorry I have choir practice this evening."

"Come on, Mike," I said. "This is important! An angry mob could form against me, and I will be there all by myself."

"I'm sorry," Mike said. "I'm already committed to serving at my church."

When I approached the hearing room on the day of the meeting, the homeowners started laughing at me, saying that the meeting had been canceled. Apparently, someone came in the middle of the night and removed the public notice signs from the property, making the meeting invalid. According to zoning regulations, the property had to be posted with the public hearing dates two weeks prior to the meeting, and because the signs had been removed from the property, the meeting had been canceled.

To make matters worse, Shiloh Group was being forced to discontinue any future involvement with me. Members from the opposition group had made repeated phone calls and complaints to the head officials at Social Services. These women were so effective at spreading their agenda that the director of Social Services called Mr. George and told him that if he didn't stop the public hearings they would cancel all his contracts and pull the kids from his care.

I'm not sure if someone from Shiloh Group removed the zoning signs or if it was someone from the neighborhood. In any event, I was left all alone facing an angry mob without any support. A part of me wanted to continue fighting the opposition group simply for the sake of moral principles, but I was outnumbered. There was a major spiritual battle raging over the sex-offender facility, and I was being attacked from every possible direction.

CHAPTER EIGHT

As I continued to pray about the next step of the process, it became very apparent to me that I needed help. I needed an army of God. I needed a church full of saints militant who would be willing to lay down their lives to fight evil. I needed an army of Catholic warriors who would take a stand for righteousness in an ungodly world. If seven sexually abused women from the opposition group could stir up such an angry mob, why couldn't a few Spirit-filled Christians raise up the necessary support to advance God's kingdom here on earth?

If an army of spiritual warriors showed up at the public zoning meeting, the opposition group wouldn't have a chance. For every sexually abused woman who wanted to vent her hurt, there could be 20 Spirit-filled women right there to love and befriend her. The saints militant could minister to the hurting women and share God's love and healing power. They could get these women to talk about their painful pasts and offer to pray with them. They could invite them to church or to their small-group communities, and by so doing, help them come out of the darkness and into the light of Christ.

Over the next several weeks, I tried to get some churches to help with the project. I asked the pastor of a church where I was attending a men's Bible study, and although he said it sounded interesting, he didn't want to get involved. The same was true for the rest of the pastors I spoke with. They were all too busy running the daily operations of their parishes. Most of these men worked 10 to 12 hours a day preparing homilies, helping children prepare for First Communion, hearing confessions, performing baptisms and marriage preparation classes, not to mention all the late-night ministry calls and trips to the hospital to anoint the sick.

The average pastor is way too busy to get involved in the affairs of our modern-day society, and it is for this reason, according to the bishops' decree, that the laity have been given the responsibility to renew the temporal order. Every aspect of the Shiloh Group project needed to be renewed through the lay apostolate of evangelization and sanctification. The entire neighborhood needed stronger Christian principles regarding the rampant spread of sexual immorality that has swept across our nation. Even the county commissioners, zoning officials, and public lawmakers needed help staying focused on solid Christian principles.

Another example of the laity's need to renew the temporal order comes from the growing number of medical marijuana dispensaries in Denver, Colorado. I first discovered this problem through advertisements in the daily newspaper. Every day new advertisements would appear with bright green marijuana leaves saying, "Get legal for only $250—Our doctors make house calls—Same day delivery of high-grade medical marijuana direct to your door."

The problems started over a decade ago when voters approved Amendment 20 to legalize medical marijuana, even though the sale of marijuana violates federal law. To make matters worse, the Obama administration said it would respect state marijuana laws when it came to federal drug enforcement. Now, according to *The Denver Post* in an article entitled "Pot Capital, USA," Denver has issued more than 300 sales tax licenses for dispensaries. *That number slightly exceeds the number of Starbucks coffee shops in Denver and surrounding areas, calculated within a 50-mile radius. It is roughly twice the number of the city's public schools. It exceeds the number of retail liquor stores in Denver by about a third.*[20]

Not only have 300 medical marijuana dispensaries opened their doors for business in the Denver area, but these dispensaries have been handing out business cards in the parking lots at public schools. In another article from *The Denver Post* entitled "Smoke and Mirrors," a drug counselor said, *"I have seen more than a dozen young people—all between the ages of 18 and 25, all with histories of substance abuse—who received from other doctors what are essentially permission slips to smoke pot."*[21]

One of his colleagues recently reported seeing a young pregnant woman who was granted a license to smoke marijuana because of her nausea. Other kids have been obtaining prescriptions to treat attention deficit disorder and hyperactivity. Not only would smoking pot make a student's attention deficit disorder worse, but according to interviews with drug counselors, *"When they're high, these young people make poor choices that lead to unplanned pregnancies, sexually transmitted diseases, school dropouts and car accidents that harm innocent people. When teenagers are withdrawing from marijuana, they can be aggressive and get into fights or instigate conflicts that lead to more trouble."*[22]

In the past, it would have been beyond comprehension that high school students could acquire a prescription to smoke pot simply by visiting one of the 15 doctors in the state who have already handed out over 10,000 prescriptions. To make matters worse, there's a growing force called the 420 movement. The term *420,* now street slang for marijuana use, was first used by a group of high school students in San Rafael, California, to refer to the time when they would meet after school to smoke dope.

As the movement continues to grow in force, hundreds of thousands of people have been gathering on April 20 to smoke pot at 4:20 p.m. The event in Denver this year made headline news with a large photograph of the state capitol building in the background. In the foreground, according to police estimates, there were 7,000 to 8,000 people smoking pot. The same event occurred last year as a protest against the war on drugs. This year, they were celebrating the medical marijuana victory. The event also included a number of booths, with doctors ready to perform evaluations, and salesmen who were handing out business cards that read, "New customers—bring this card in for a free gram!"

As the entire world continues to plummet down the slippery slope of moral and spiritual depravity, the bishops' call for action has become even more imperative: *Laymen ought to take on themselves as their distinctive task this renewal of the temporal order. Guided by the light of the Gospel and the mind of the Church, prompted by Christian love, they should act in this domain in a direct way and in their own specific manner.*[23]

CHAPTER NINE

Charitable Works and Social Aid

To be effective in a lay apostolate, the faithful will need to operate in all three categories, including those of charitable works and social aid to the poor. According to the bishops' decree, *Wherever men are to be found who are in want of food and drink, of clothing, housing, medicine, work, education, the means necessary for leading a truly human life, wherever there are men racked by misfortune or illness, men suffering exile or imprisonment, Christian charity should go in search of them and find them out, comfort them with devoted care and give them the helps that will relieve their needs. This obligation binds first and foremost the more affluent individuals and nations.*[24]

According to the bishops' decree, the laity can fulfill their apostolic duties by working together in groups, individually, or as a family unit. When I first heard about the family apostolate, I was concerned that it would reflect a secular perspective—that husbands need to spend more time with their wives—that wives need to be more understanding and attentive to their husbands, and the kids—well the kids just need more of everything: more attention, toys, music, video games, and cell phones.

Unlike the family dynamics of our modern-day society, the bishops present a different view for the family apostolate by recommending the following forms of action: *Adopting abandoned children, showing a loving welcome to strangers, helping with the running of schools, supporting adolescents with advice and help, assisting engaged couples to make a better preparation for marriage, taking a share in catechism-teaching, supporting married people and families in a material or moral crisis, and in the case of the aged, not only providing them with what is indispensable, but also procuring for them a fair share of the fruits of economic progress.*[25]

When families spend all their time and resources on themselves, all it seems to produce is selfish kids. But when families participate in a lay apostolate, their children grow up being missionary minded. When children are taught about the different countries in the world and spend their time before meals praying for missionaries in those countries, they have a better chance of growing up to become missionaries themselves.

When families spend a day a week providing food for the hungry, visiting the elderly, and proclaiming the Gospel message, their children have a better chance of embracing their faith. A large number of Catholic youth today have been walking away from the faith because they were forced to participate in what they consider "meaningless religious behaviors." Their faith was never encouraged or brought to life in a meaningful way through the family apostolate.

In addition to the family apostolate, all Catholics are required to participate in their own individual apostolates. According to the bishops' decree, *The individual apostolate is everywhere and always in place; in certain circumstances it is the only one appropriate, the only one possible. Every lay person, whatever his condition, is called to it, is obliged to it.*[26]

A good example of how the individual apostolate operates comes from a typical visit to the grocery store. If while standing in line, I were to encounter another shopper who looked troubled, through the inspiration and power of the Holy Spirit, I should reach out to that person with the love of Christ. In these types of situations, it may not be possible to find a priest or a more experienced member of a prayer team for help, so for this reason, the individual apostolate is everywhere and always in place.

Maybe the best ways to minister to another shopper in this situation would be to invite that person to a small-group, fellowship meeting. In an apostolic exhortation entitled, *Evangelii Nuntiandi,* Pope Paul VI makes reference to small-group communities as an excellent way for the laity to carry out their apostolate. Small-group communities work in conjunction with the mission of the whole Church, except they are designed to be a more intimate setting for Catholics to learn and grow in their faith.

Almost anyone can start a small-group community simply by inviting a few friends over to their house for a Bible study or a fellowship meeting. Once the members form a solid core-team that meets on a regular basis, they can open up the group to others for evangelization. If I were to meet a distressed shopper in the grocery store, I could invite that person to my small-group fellowship meeting. In this type of setting, the distressed shopper would have the opportunity to learn more about the Catholic faith and also to open up to others about the problems that he or she may be experiencing.

The same type of small-group community is also an excellent way to evangelize members of non-Christian religions. For example, if I were to meet a Muslim man at the grocery store, I could invite him to the fellowship meeting by asking him to speak about Islam. If the group was organized in a way where different members presented a different teaching every week, I could invite him over the first week to meet everybody and listen to a message about love. Maybe the second week, another member of the group could talk about forgiveness. On the third week, after the Muslim man had a chance to learn more about the teachings of Christ, he could share his views on Islam.

It is through these types of fellowship meetings, backed by the power of prayer and the Holy Spirit, that the laity will be able to grow in their faith while fulfilling the Great Commission.

In regards to Catholics working together with non-Catholics or even non-Christians, it would be important to note that under a heading entitled, Co-operation with other Christians and Non-Christians, the bishops say that it is *desirable, and often imperative, that Catholics cooperate with other Christians.*[27] Through this dynamic, yet prudent, cooperation, which is of great importance in temporal activities, the laity bears witness to Christ the Saviour of the world, and to the unity of the human family.[28]

According to the bishops' decree, in union with Pope Paul VI, under the inspiration of the Holy Spirit, the Council, then, makes to all the laity an earnest appeal in the Lord to give a willing, noble and enthusiastic response to the voice of Christ, who at this hour is summoning them more pressingly, and to the urging of the Holy Spirit. The younger generation should feel this call to be addressed in a special way to themselves; they should welcome it eagerly and generously. It is the Lord himself, by this Council, who is once more inviting all the laity to unite themselves to him even more intimately, to consider his interests as their own, and to join in his mission as Saviour.[29]

CHAPTER TEN

Another way for the laity to fulfill their calling in Christ is through a simple, three-part process that was taught by Jesus and lived out in the lives of the apostles. The first step occurs when we surrender our lives unto the Lord's service. The second step comes about by listening to the Lord's guidance through contemplative prayer, and the third step is obedience. It is through this simple, three-part process that the Lord uses his servants to advance his kingdom here on earth.

This three-part process was first described in a parable concerning our need to build a solid spiritual house on rock. In Luke 6:46–49, Jesus says, *"Why do you call me 'Lord, Lord,' and do not do what I tell you? I will show you what someone is like who comes to me, hears my words, and acts on them. That one is like a man building a house, who dug deeply and laid the foundation on rock; when a flood arose, the river burst against that house but could not shake it, because it had been well built. But the one who hears and does not act is like a man who built a house on the ground without a foundation. When the river burst against it, immediately it fell, and great was the ruin of that house."*

The first step of surrender is described in the first verse where Jesus says, "Why do you call me 'Lord, Lord' and do not do what I tell you?" In order to make Jesus the Lord of your life, it will be necessary to surrender your life unto his service. The second and third steps are contained in the second verse where Jesus says, "I will show you what someone is like who comes to me, *hears* my words, and *acts* on them." The second step of listening is defined by our need to *hear* the Lord's words. This third step of obedience is fulfilled by our *actions* when we complete the assignments that he gives us.

The same three-part process has also been demonstrated for us in the lives of the apostles. In Acts 9:10–12, *there was a disciple in Damascus named Ananias. The Lord said to him in a vision, "Ananias." He answered, "Here I am, Lord." The Lord said to him, "Get up and go to the street called Straight, and at the house of Judas look for a man of Tarsus named Saul. At this moment he is praying, and he has seen in a vision a man named Ananias come in and lay his hands on him so that he might regain his sight."*

In this situation, we see the Lord communicating with his servant through prayer. Ananias is already a surrendered servant of the Lord and is waiting to receive his next ministry assignment. When the Lord speaks to him, Ananias is willing to listen. Ananias is practicing a form of contemplative prayer where he is able to listen to the Lord from the depths of his heart. After he receives his next assignment, we see Ananias raising an objection in Acts 9:13–16:

> *But Ananias answered, "Lord, I have heard from many about this man, how much evil he has done to your saints in Jerusalem; and here he has authority from the chief priests to bind all who invoke your name." But the Lord said to him, "Go, for he is an instrument whom I have chosen to bring my name before Gentiles and kings and before the people of Israel; I myself will show him how much he must suffer for the sake of my name."*

Even though Ananias is a surrendered servant of the Lord, willing to accomplish anything the Lord asks, we still see a need for a deeper form of surrender. In this situation, the Lord was calling Ananias into a situation that could be very dangerous. Paul already had Steven stoned to death, and after obtaining authority to arrest those who considered themselves Christian, he was traveling to Damascus looking for more people to persecute.

It's understandable why Ananias would be concerned for his safety. The men Paul was traveling with could have arrested him and sent him to prison. Even though Ananias had to put his own life in jeopardy, we see him surrender his fears and concerns to the Lord and proceed forth in obedience. In Acts 9:17–19, *Ananias went and entered the house. He laid his hands on Saul and said, "Brother Saul, the Lord Jesus, who appeared to you on your way here, has sent me so that you may regain your sight and be filled with the Holy Spirit." And immediately something like scales fell from his eyes, and his sight was restored. Then he got up and was baptized, and after taking some food, he regained his strength.*

It was by following the three-part process of surrender, listening, and obedience that Ananias was able to fulfill his missionary assignment. It was also through this process that the miracle-working power of God was released. Through Ananias's apostolate, Paul regained his sight, was filled with the Holy Spirit, and was baptized into the Christian faith.

Another example of how this three-part process was able to release the miracle-working power of God comes from the life of Peter. In Acts 10:2–6, there was a man from Caesarea named Cornelius. *He was a devout man who feared God with all his household; he gave alms generously to the people and prayed constantly to God.*

One afternoon at about three o'clock he had a vision in which he clearly saw an angel of God coming in and saying to him, "Cornelius." He stared at him in terror and said, "What is it, Lord?" He answered, "Your prayers and your alms have ascended as a memorial before God. Now send men to Joppa for a certain Simon who is called Peter; he is lodging with Simon, a tanner, whose house is by the seaside."

Peter had no idea that Cornelius would send men in search of him, and even if he did, he probably would not have traveled with them because they were Gentiles. Peter, being obedient to the Jewish purification rituals, wasn't allowed to eat with or enter the house of a Gentile. Because God wanted Peter to make disciples of all nations, by spreading the Gospel message even to the Gentiles, he required a deeper form of surrender and obedience.

In Acts 10:9–20, *As they were on their journey and approaching the city, Peter went up on the roof to pray. He became hungry and wanted something to eat; and while it was being prepared, he fell into a trance.*

He saw the heaven opened and something like a large sheet coming down, being lowered to the ground by its four corners. In it were all kinds of four-footed creatures and reptiles and birds of the air. Then he heard a voice saying, "Get up, Peter; kill and eat." But Peter said, "By no means, Lord; for I have never eaten anything that is profane or unclean." The voice said to him again, a second time, "What God has made clean, you must not call profane." This happened three times, and the thing was suddenly taken up to heaven.

Now while Peter was greatly puzzled about what to make of the vision that he had seen, suddenly the men sent by Cornelius appeared. They were asking for Simon's house and were standing by the gate. They called out to ask whether Simon, who was called Peter, was staying there. While Peter was still thinking about the vision, the Spirit said to him, "Look, three men are searching for you. Now get up, go down, and go with them without hesitation; for I have sent them."

In this situation, we see Peter having a conversation with the Lord. He is communicating with the Lord through prayer and listening to the Lord's instructions. Even though Peter is a surrendered servant of the Lord, he still needs a deeper form of submission by surrendering his prejudice attitude toward the Gentiles. After Peter received his instructions through listening, and released his fears and concerns through surrender, he proceeded to carry out his missionary assignment in obedience.

Upon entering Cornelius's house the following day, Peter proclaimed the Gospel message to a large group of Gentiles who had gathered. *While Peter was still speaking, the Holy Spirit fell upon all who heard the word. The circumcised believers who had come with Peter were astounded that the gift of the Holy Spirit had been poured out even on the Gentiles, for they heard them speaking in tongues and extolling God. Then Peter said, "Can anyone withhold the water for baptizing these people who have received the Holy Spirit just as we have?" So he ordered them to be baptized in the name of Jesus Christ. Then they invited him to stay for several days.*[30]

It was through the three-part process of surrender, listening, and obedience that the miracle-working power of God was released into the lives of the Gentile converts. After the Holy Spirit descended upon Cornelius's household, Peter stayed with them several more days to teach them the fullness of the faith. In the same way Peter was able to make converts out of the Gentiles, so too, are all Catholics required to make disciples of all nations.

CHAPTER ELEVEN

The process of accomplishing God's will for your life begins with a full and complete surrender unto the Lord's service. Sacred Scripture offers many different examples for this type of relationship that Jesus desires from all his followers. In John 10:27, Jesus presents himself as the Good Shepherd by saying, *"My sheep hear my voice. I know them, and they follow me."* One of the characteristics of sheep is their dependence on the shepherd. Sheep submit themselves unto the shepherd's care, they know how to listen to the shepherd's voice, and they follow him in obedience.

Goats on the other hand are stubborn and rebellious. They don't like following the shepherd's directives. They would rather pursue their own selfish interests and passions in life, oftentimes to their own peril. The same is true in our relationship with the Good Shepherd. We have the choice of acting like rebellious goats, pursuing our own self-willed agendas, or we can lay down our lives to serve the Lord.

Surrender

The process of surrendering your life unto the Lord's service is a lifelong journey. At different points in a person's life, the Lord may require different forms of surrender. He may ask that you surrender 10 percent of your income as a tithe to help advance his kingdom. He may require you to surrender your sex life, or give up the pursuit of romance and marriage so that you may serve him more completely. The Good Shepherd may ask that you start serving him in ministry one day a week. He may even allow you to experience severe hardships in life to get your attention, so that after you have given up on your self-willed ways, you may enter into his service more completely.

Those who lay down a small percentage of their lives into his service will quickly discover that Jesus will require more and more, until finally he is Lord and Master over every aspect of your life. Jesus wants your full devotion. He requires a full and complete surrender from all of his followers. In Matthew 10:37–39, Jesus says, *"Whoever loves father or mother more than me is not worthy of me; and whoever loves son or daughter more than me is not worthy of me; and whoever does not take up the cross and follow me is not worthy of me. Those who find their life will lose it, and those who lose their life for my sake will find it."*

Listening

The process of listening to the softly spoken voice of the Lord begins by developing a contemplative prayer life. Prayer is communion with God, similar to a two-way conversation where one person talks and the other person listens. The problem with most forms of prayer is that everybody wants to talk, and nobody wants to listen.

In order to develop a deeper contemplative prayer life, it will be helpful to remove all the noisy distractions from your life, so that you can quiet your internal dialog long enough to hear the Lord speak. I began this process several years ago for Lent by offering to give up television in exchange for a deeper prayer life.

I used to watch several hours of television every evening. Because I didn't have cable, I used to flip back and forth between channels until my ten o'clock bedtime. On the first day of Lent, I prayed for as long as I could and ended up going to bed around 7:30 p.m. I didn't know how to pray, except for reciting a few rote prayers over and over again.

As the days of Lent progressed, I was able to develop a sweet intimacy with the Lord during my prayer time. I started talking to Jesus like a personal friend. I got very real with him about every aspect of my life. On many evenings, I would take blankets outside and lay in my hammock looking up at the star-filled night sky. I would ask God all kinds of questions, and after basking in the Lord's glorious presence for several hours, the answers would simply enter my consciousness.

In the Catechism of the Catholic Church, Saint Teresa describes this type of prayer life by saying, *"Contemplative prayer in my opinion is nothing else than a close sharing between friends; it means taking time frequently to be alone with him who we know loves us.*

Contemplative prayer seeks him whom my soul loves. It is Jesus, and in him, the Father. We seek him, because to desire him is always the beginning of love, and we seek him in that pure faith which causes us to be born of him and to live in him."[31]

Contemplative prayer is hearing the Word of God. Far from being passive, such attentiveness is the obedience of faith, the unconditional acceptance of a servant, and the loving commitment of a child.[32] Contemplative prayer is silence, the symbol of the world to come or silent love. Words in this kind of prayer are not speeches; they are like kindling that feeds the fire of love.[33]

The best way to begin the process of practicing contemplative prayer is by removing all the noisy distractions from your life. Set aside several hours every evening simply to be in the Lord's presence. Talk to him from the depths of your heart and ponder the answers that he will give you in your spirit. It is through the process of a contemplative prayer life that you will be able to listen to and discern the softly spoken voice of the Lord.

Obedience

Once you hear from the Lord on the direction that he wants you to pursue in life, the next step is obedience. Those who are serious about following the Lord wherever he leads will quickly discover that his plans for your life may be in direct conflict with the ways of the world. There may even be times when the Lord's will for your life may appear frightening or downright dangerous. In the Gospel of Matthew, Jesus made the disciples get into a boat and cross the sea of Galilee ahead of him while he dismissed the

crowds. Very early in the morning, the disciples saw
a ghostly figure walking toward them on the water.
They were terrified, but Jesus called out to them saying, *"Take heart, it is I; do not be afraid."*

*Peter answered him, "Lord, if it is you, command me
to come to you on the water."*

He said, "Come."

*So Peter got out of the boat, started walking on the
water, and came toward Jesus. But when he noticed the
strong wind, he became frightened, and beginning to
sink, he cried out, "Lord, save me!"*

*Jesus immediately reached out his hand and caught
him, saying to him, "You of little faith, why did you
doubt?" When they got into the boat, the wind ceased.
And those in the boat worshiped him, saying, "Truly you
are the Son of God."*[34]

In the same way the Lord granted Peter permission to step out of the boat and walk on water, so too,
may he ask the rest of his followers to do things that
seem totally contrary to the ways of the world. No
fisherman in his right mind would climb out of his
boat in an attempt to walk on water, but when you
have the Lord Jesus guiding your ministry endeavors,
all that is required is steadfast faith and obedience.

After you surrender your situation unto the Lord,
listen carefully to his softly spoken voice and proceed
forth in obedience, you will need to start the process
all over again. In Peter's case, the lack of faith caused
him to sink. The same thing may occur in the lives of
the rest of the Lord's followers. When this happens,

it's important to start the process all over again. Surrender your fears unto the Lord, ask for his forgiveness, take hold of his hand, and listen to what he has to say. After receiving your next set of instructions, you'll need to proceed forth in obedience.

Step-by-step the Lord will lead and guide every aspect of your life, relationships, and ministry endeavors.

CHAPTER TWELVE

Become a Catholic Lay Evangelist

One of the best ways to fulfill your calling as a Catholic lay evangelist is to start spiritual conversations about God with other people. Instead of asking people awkward questions like, "If you were to die today, where would you go?" try a more natural approach by incorporating spiritual topics into your daily conversations.

To begin this process, simply invite the Holy Spirit to join your daily interactions. Spend a lot of time listening to what other people have to say. Once you find some common ground between the other person's beliefs and your own, try sharing some of the Lord's teachings with them, or some of the spiritual principles behind the Sacraments. By doing so, you will be fulfilling your calling as a Catholic lay evangelist.

Start a Small-Group Fellowship

One of the best ways to begin the process of

advancing God's kingdom is by setting up a small-group fellowship meeting. In the same way that it's important for all Catholics to attend Mass on Sunday, it's also important for every Catholic to have a place where they can learn and grow in their faith, share personal struggles, discuss topics, and help others draw closer to Christ.

To start a small-group, all you need to do is invite a few friends over for a weekly fellowship meeting. Possible directions for the group could include a Bible study, a prayer and praise service, or just a fellowship meeting where different members present a study topic every week. Once you establish a solid core group, it will become an excellent environment to invite new believers or other people from your community, so that you can help them grow in their faith.

Embark on a Mission Trip

Embarking on a mission trip is a great way to deepen your love for the poor. In many underdeveloped countries, the majority of the residents are living in wooden shacks or huts made out of adobe. In other situations, you may encounter starving children living in a trash dump. Even though the majority of people in Third-World countries don't have running water or electricity, they are usually the kindest, most hospitable people you'll ever meet.

By visiting a Third-World country, not only will you have many opportunities to present the teachings of Christ to others, but when you encounter the hardships that other people are facing throughout the world, the Lord will be able to teach you a lot of things about yourself. It is through the process of deepening your love for other people that you will be able to more effectively advance the kingdom of heaven here on earth.

Develop the Proper Attitude

In 1 Corinthians 9:24–27, Saint Paul discloses the proper attitude for a Catholic lay evangelist by saying, *"Do you not know that in a race the runners all compete, but only one receives the prize? Run in such a way that you may win it. Athletes exercise self-control in all things; they do it to receive a perishable wreath, but we an imperishable one. So I do not run aimlessly, nor do I box as though beating the air; but I punish my body and enslave it, so that after proclaiming to others I myself should not be disqualified."*

In order to excel in your ministry endeavors, it will be necessary to run the race like Saint Paul. When you first start out, your ministry assignments may seem small and insignificant. But when you continue your training, giving your best to God, you will progressively receive more spiritual power and responsibilities. The more you receive, the more the Lord will require from you, until eventually, you will grow rich advancing the kingdom of heaven here on earth.

Pray to Be More Effective

In Matthew 9:35–38, *Jesus went about all the cities and villages, teaching in their synagogues, and proclaiming the good news of the kingdom, and curing every disease and every sickness. When he saw the crowds, he had compassion for them, because they were harassed and helpless, like sheep without a shepherd. Then he said to his disciples, "The harvest is plentiful, but the laborers are few; therefore ask the Lord of the harvest to send out laborers into his harvest."*

In the same way that Jesus went about proclaiming the good news and ministering to those who were hurting, so too are all Catholics called to follow his example. Not only is it important to pray for an increased missionary activity within the Church, but to pray for the safety and productivity of all missionaries throughout the world. It will also be helpful to pray for your own apostolate by asking the Lord to remove anything from your life that is preventing you from advancing his kingdom more passionately.

Go Beyond the Call of Duty

According to Sacred Scripture, the Lord's servants are required to plow the fields and tend the sheep. The fields represent the world, and those who work in the fields spend their time making disciples of all nations. The flock represents the Church, and those who spend their time tending the sheep work in the Church helping others grow closer to Christ.

In Luke 17:7–10 Jesus says, *"Who among you would say to your slave who has just come in from plowing or tending sheep in the field, 'Come here at once and take your place at the table'? Would you not rather say to him, 'Prepare supper for me, put on your apron and serve me while I eat and drink; later you may eat and drink'? Do you thank the slave for doing what was commanded? So you also, when you have done all that you were ordered to do, say, 'We are worthless slaves; we have done only what we ought to have done!'"*

Whether you work as a Catholic lay evangelist in the fields or minister to the lambs within the flock, we are all required to go beyond the call of duty by giving our best to God.

Take Action Immediately

If you are waiting on God to call you into ministry, it may never happen. God has already given us everything we need to know in Sacred Scripture. God wants us to use our free will in making a choice to serve him. Once we make a choice to fulfill the Great Commission, it will be helpful to follow the advice of the greatest missionary of all time:

In 2 Timothy 4:1–5, Saint Paul says, *"I solemnly urge you: proclaim the message; be persistent whether the time is favorable or unfavorable; convince, rebuke, and encourage, with the utmost patience in teaching. For the time is coming when people will not put up with sound doctrine, but having itching ears, they will accumulate for themselves teachers to suit their own desires, and will turn away from listening to the truth and wander away to myths. As for you, always be sober, endure suffering, do the work of an evangelist, carry out your ministry fully."*

1. Acts 14:8–13.

2. Acts 14:14–15 & 18.

3. United States Department of State, *Travel Warning* (Washington, DC: Bureau of Consular Affairs). Effective on July 17, 2009, www.travel.state.gov.

4. United States Department of State, *Travel Warning*.

5. Acts 2:38–39.

6. Catechism of the Catholic Church: 1265; *2 Cor* 5:17; *2 Pet* 1:4; cf. *Gal* 4:5–7; cf. *1 Cor* 6:15; 12:27; *Rom* 8:17; cf. *1 Cor* 6:19.

7. Catechism of the Catholic Church: 1256; CIC, can. 861 § 2.

8. Catechism of the Catholic Church: 1250; cf. CIC, can. 867; CCEO, cann. 681; 686, 1.

9. Matthew 28:18–20.

10. Luke 10:17–19.

11. Catechism of the Catholic Church: Glossary, p. 875.

12. Catechism of the Catholic Church: Glossary, p. 866.

13. Catechism of the Catholic Church: Glossary, p. 867.

14. Austin Flannery, O.P., *Vatican Council II, Vatican Collection Volume 1, The Conciliar and Post Conciliar Documents, New Revised Edition* (Collegeville, MN: Liturgical Press, 1975 and 1984) p. 766.

15. Austin Flannery, O.P., *Vatican Council II,* p. 768.

16. Austin Flannery, O.P., *Vatican Council II,* p. 767.

17. Austin Flannery, O.P., *Vatican Council II,* p. 773, cf. *Mt* 5:16.

18. Austin Flannery, O.P., *Vatican Council II,* p. 773.

19. Austin Flannery, O.P., *Vatican Council II,* p. 773.

20. Christopher N. Osher, "Pot Capital, U.S.A.," *The Denver Post* (Denver, CO, January 3, 2010) p. 1A.

21. Christian Thurstone, "Smoke and Mirrors," *The Denver Post* (Denver, CO, January 31, 2010) p. 1D.

22. Christian Thurstone, "Smoke and Mirrors," p. 6D.

23. Austin Flannery, O.P., *Vatican Council II,* p. 774.

24. Austin Flannery, O.P., *Vatican Council II,* p. 776.

25. Austin Flannery, O.P., *Vatican Council II,* p. 779.

26. Austin Flannery, O.P., *Vatican Council II,* p. 783.

27. Austin Flannery, O.P., *Vatican Council II,* p. 792.

28. Austin Flannery, O.P., *Vatican Council II,* p. 792.

29. Austin Flannery, O.P., *Vatican Council II,* p. 797, cf. *Phil* 2:5.

30. Acts 10:44–48.

31. Catechism of the Catholic Church: 2709; St. Teresa of Jesus, *The Book of Her Life,* 8, 5 in *The Collected Works of St. Teresa of Avila,* tr. K. Kavanaugh, OCD, and O. Rodriguez, OCD (Washington, DC: Institute of Carmelite Studies, 1976), I, 67; *Song* 1:7; cf. 3:1–4.

32. Catechism of the Catholic Church: 2716.

33. Catechism of the Catholic Church: 2717; cf. St. Isaac of Nineveh, *Tract. myst.* 66; St. John of the Cross, *Maxims and Counsels,* 53 in *The Collected Works of St. John of the Cross,* tr. K. Kavanaugh, OCD, and O. Rodriguez, OCD (Washington, DC: Institute of Carmelite Studies, 1979), 678.

34. Matthew 14:27–33.

About the Author

Robert Abel's purpose and passion in life is speaking God's truth unto today's generation. He lives in Denver, Colorado, where he leads a homeless ministry and conducts mission trips to Africa.

If you would like to join Robert on the next mission trip, or would like him to speak at your parish, please contact:

www.AfricaMissionaries.com

If you would like to participate in our evangelization ministry, please consider spreading the message from *Worldwide Adventure*. To purchase additional copies of this book for ministry purposes, or to make a donation, please use the following information:

Number of Copies	Ministry Price
6	$29
12	$49
18	$69

These prices include tax and shipping within the United States. For shipments to other countries, please contact us. Thank you for your generous support.

Mail your payment to:

Valentine Publishing House
Worldwide Adventure
P.O. Box 27422
Denver, Colorado 80227